tv   eye

tv   eye

Todd Baron

chax press 2004

ISBN 0925904-33-3

Library of Congress Cataloging-in-Publication Data

The author would like to thank the editors and publishers of
Hambone, The Art of Practice: 45 Poets (Poets and Poet Press),
Windhover, and *Isobongo* for their work with some of these poems.

Chax Press
101 W. Sixth Street
Tucson, Arizona 85701-1000
USA

To Sophie and Michele —
without whom, which,
what? without—

contents

`

tv

tv

suitability

((for Allen Ginsberg))

the key is in the window,
the key is in the sunlight
in the window.

jupiter

The body opens
interrupted by dust
Define a potential
as if the angle of condition
concealed this central
permance / continuance
not a parity

hyphen

(for Fanny Howe)

I translate into fear like this
— small iridescent
worn life (this
ink
laying by the field
in the use of hands —
Every angel is terrifying
— like milk in the morning
or sky

dusk

as though again you are traveling light
and loving the vision of courtly love
whose voice is capable
and that they had
what they came for
had been together
been pulled apart
the pluralistic comprehends
channels of agreement
based on whom will call
the unseen troops
or master of partitions
the walls have sea walls
and the same city's been bombed
four times now but who doesn't care
for their lots are sand and wind
& this warm regiment sails
into the obliquely
political zone

means

antipodes in some bright sacrosanct
exile formally a human
head with a hole
that moves with the tops of trees
always filled with trees
and concrete sound

division

for example the tempo is bitter the complexity
while rain grew was heard to
her intelligence your clairvoyance
was invented to help people
franchise the most sovereign
body *in morbid detail*
and to refresh myself I directed men and women
to find money
& rethinking and reading the lock
until the color of speech
or imagination sees
organized crossing and recrossing
lost labor

howl

great big wail of no money
like gardens in pastures
howling down

I, primarily

a focused uncertainty
a function of the persister
varying reductions or minds
process witness
during a sequence valved
knowingly to determine
field & war's economy

embassy

I've no idea whether justice is love
or just a vibration the relativity of
measurements into our own
categories transported
jobs or loss of what they command
as much as any research does
the lost
       labor's
emanations substitute a word
why she wrote are there
male/female detectives the months
escape from memory
       leafless things are mazes
closed & folded
study the insurrection the scene
at night watching the
            corroding horizontal

reason

Because that's the way
it is down here
roaming as it were
a valley striving to be
the other side of a ditch
that I saw and was
attracted to but how
change not the will
to balance *the body*
or spell the in-
correct thing
in light of
distrust &
music
        cried
that the number of adjectives
used a bat tonight

allowance

the softer music
at the edge
& notes surrounded by
    shade
& all that green
cloud or chains slipping
the bunker

lyric: gesture

there night blades seek
the edge of the bed
as windows spurning east
from asterisks unable to say
even the slightest thing about
real life as they do
At the onset of looking
into the room filled with people
with people he says
alone at this note
disregarding
only the fictive

radio

       I have an idea
that ink bleeds through the page
earlier radios renounce
one would say God as objects
not listening to themselves
who use them function solely
on what should be called
indenting thumbprint
where warring factions would
follow the public
undisclosed record and recording
message the gun
facing the other
only such smaller and less
economic or loving circles
to the dark
troth
when you least want
the in ability to love

netting

half a doubled
subordinate in the
realm of superstition
my father's chair
in a sub-
canticle of light
the figure
sooner or later forgets
which world is real
in the later dodging
negative electric
choral

return

the cage overgrown the sound
now a film from primary weeds
and savings droned inedible fruit
even if it's not words
the color of ink & time (& page
elevated under strings
& all those movements of some small
body from which the face
if anything is forgotten

those few reaches

this is really this   higher
alright than before
muscular sensations or
a matter of adeptness//apprenticeship
the inanimate past missing
gesticulating muscle
in the back of distance round
cursing lines growing
beside a fallen indentation now
tomorrow
dropped

two prayers

be trothed
with good faith binding
householders form permanent
person to pay money with that
open-air distance
through the woods
stammering
stuttering in both
senses humming

[lear]

        with a bolt
of good faire so that
we spoke in celebration (cotton
proceeds the earliest sale *MAKE IT?*
I can't even walk with you
row of lights dates
configured the municipality
he said that
words reproduce the same
                   social
origin earliest from clef
to cliff the trifolium
areola
above the arches
string –and-key
of a rhetorical period I mean
HOW DO YOU GET IN
the lot of this ministry?
men's garb

under head and action
 asks
    fetter?
try tying one down
try call-waiting
when you write
to a bird
his wing-spread song
Do scald like a molten lead

7pm

hence our position to run
to silence is left, now
speak to me of the turtle
I want to be where what you say
is what you wear
but the future set by meandering devices
the normalcy of talk (like)
things in the middle

moderate duration

still nothing wind's tree subterfuge
light compass situations work the tree's
demand scanning long shelves
blots patternless pleats grow
like grotto leaves letters
birds the breakdown
of direction *I see my*
own mistake and
when I say hours
 dear sensual solid letter
I mean years
significations past blind dates
dense geometry illustration
the emancipated state bewildered
smoldering norm

discontinuation

which is beautiful and of the earth
Streaming a cell
that is—
contained by other largeness—
by its own process
not discreet but stirring
outmoded
branches

are

what would you do
in the morning moving
like an adversary
to paint a picture of
the skies who wait
across the bed
in some degree
of this free world

coarse house

mother please don't bury me
the nest is in the kitchen
& the flower's
about to burn the bomb
too is a giant derma
replete with homilies strange
you never knew
how invented lives
were and now
forms build light
where parts deflect
on that patio
or what we call the patio
between your legs
because there's nothing else
but this brown
milk & this dream
deflated *as a piece of skin*
forced to sit outside
our own experience

to watch the weather
stain the house
and the workers
in a seemingly endless
stain of events
perpetuated by cause
& the lack of function
O don't wither me down
so fantastic that the rafters
support a slope
keening from the
main bribe
          talk to me
as a glib rain
falls so rare
in this part of
the neighborhood
that when the phone rings
you pick it up
from so much heat

spaced

which solicit me
under the name transformed
to a pitch
                    if I have the gift
alright, we'll give
it a chance this
experience but anxiety'
s the same she's
the sister of a brother
I, fervor,
            lost
delicately
because I want to say
less is oblique
domesticating vision
determining factor
leaving innate surface
the ballot shifts

swear not

love *is* love
never mind the owner
(never mind the dog)
beware the owner
if instead of seeing them
below you saw them *below*
and the drift followed
a pelagic association
like (when) like
when you said
I have nothing to doubt
but driving one
of those fast books
you
we divorced your-
self
from turning the page
no matter what you've read
it's being read continually
& there's tape
in the window

herald

(for n.c.)

it doesn't matter
 what thought this is
only that the rhythm of the thing
the arena moves
as the element suffers
barred otherwise
as though we were there—
—that the movement of anything at all
(we are there) suffers (that isn't us)
nor the composition of the task
in reference to the shape
or message

horses

she just loved me in sequence
& even that shows forward thinking
his sign comes true the sign
I'm not saying I could call anywhere—but
that the line will always be open
you make the jurors have
that kind of rough
connection but each sin or
aspect of sin as the correlation
of the unattended

the setting

it was the movement the words days
and days—repetition
the pages turn, the eye inset
what it wanted imitation
the lens sought to stick
ink sick and the inscape
her mother wanted
like she but he wanted
to break off the past the same
time judge had written
life is neither to break
nor sit in circumference
I'm jealous as the real
questioner   black on black
the partition or screen
who is none or
little as others

traditional

there is nothing like the
sequence in circumference or form
the bullet the rise
of its shape at the door

academy

how know the eclipse
of instruction how
rate the solidly confirmed picture
from that bank that bleeds

mediation

I'll be out of town next week,
but if you change the channel (& record
your number as time
we'd function past
frugality—another way past praxis—
just a thought to get us through
an involuntary image
but anything can be turned
into a picture and vice-versa
that last thought
before burning my night
Cocteau wrote "Goering's
mad laugh . . . "

aurora

what any one of us
detects are inside
of us and wakes
 at times
what one reads
or happens on the relative
statement in-
tuitive radical
mass
as places are

water

the other side of insensible
still
transmitted
hypothesis
between remote and route
circumstantial perpendicular
supposedly liturgical fields

coitus

this is a life this photograph
this parcel
posted
shine on
o harvest

camouflage

carrying these weights
over each circle
like chalkboard portions
'cross a stream into
penciled drawings
motivation quick & repellent
frost in my first sentence
this is my first sentence
because of flight & fire
on the water fuselage
in the middle of
some project for the color
grey ((gray))

compass

the purpose is to say
there's a difference
in beginning
 the machine
in what it knows
has a different
middle
light for an end

entrada

if the army could be political
music playing in the other room
while the room's asleep
and they read while
the music's like a ship
and someone starts singing
where things fall
and are recovered
and blue objects rush
at their feet
like bipartisan
flowers

itch

to be lost in the string
of the head the do it yourself
bullet-proof paper vest
serving the quiet right
tossing an impenetrable
little square where itchy
corollary to myself
the light of obligatorily
marked
posthumous skin

a corner in wheat

the clarity of the leaves
belies the instigation
of the cause   tongues
react as if they were
mountains of gears
there is no tradition
for the clocks in our heads
nor the end of talking

blues

criminal terminology
receives a text
like lakes replacing the self
but what if all that from which I awoke
or not to be delighted at curfew
all sciences form the eye
from disillusioned locks
or money

precinct

back away
and nothing
but the American
dead mark
in decay
 the zoo's a place
where I'd take the eros
like a self
medicated
member

advance

a glass of water
lights the world
the film lights
the glass of water

a variation

(for & after John Wieners)

I will be an old man somewhere
& live in dark room somewhere
by a t.v. screen I will think
of this night, as often
as not—rain or earth
falling on stone.
There will be no one
on the street,
only this song,
wanting nothing but the longing to be
apathetic with you(my
central self together on this street
Now is a time
This, chance
not the last chance
but the least
However you lay
serene, & come again
Bear me to seed,
there is no return
from this room addressed
to this room compressing your face
at the mirror

[[you]]

1

and if you want to live longer
you'll have to eat the right cereal
soil and climate
the rest of the world
preconditions exists
in iron & gold helmets a really great script
in small mountain towns
flows in the middle of your head
protrudes onto each other's intervals
gold antennas the ruins of side effects
in an almost indefinable sense
of its own marked beauty
marked by god
and the opposing batters

2

or that everyone dies like they mean something to me
headlights in shadows the majesty of film
like the majesty of film
or time or the unequivocal season
like the mail's here and it's really
musical notes and vibrations beneath my feet
a plot towards persona
like who'll speak like I am
pronouns or birds left for eligible seasons
on board computes the tail fins
of a really great cloud
or what seems to be another extension
towards the sea
crossed with salt
& the bodies at sea

3

your product unwashed
in the alignment of light
that pool of back-lit
blue water a vestige of words
named duplicity because the name
says the cadence
of the sentence that the
sentence repeats, like
alright I'll get
it somehow
the shape of the curve
the curve of the S
& the like sense of the smell
of wet soap
in the shape of (you)r hand

4

so you thought you were waking
from what (you) thought
was the smell of the weed
or the word for the
smell of the weed
but it's not really like that
people congregate
as if that were the word
but years later
they're dead
unable to congregate
as if that were word
or the people

5

it's the draining of waste
that blames it on the painting
the painting that blames it
on the hypothesis
growing out of pipes and remainders
transfigured to the shape
of an idea, yeah
an idea out of shape
or scope into
digital sound
chained to another shape
or sound of an image
let's face it
we mean
what we indicate
we indicate
what we sound

6

so that the name the absence
anyone in hand the narrative
the door and the table
intent in sleeping
in the park getting all
fucked up in the landscape
or the landscape drawn
to flipping the stage
the allusion of space
and water drawn
from an inky age
of treason and tiled sinks
and formica
as if they were
assigned to teach
the indefinite object
ideally the slope
of a lawn
or useless migration

7

the song lit a fire the song had a day
dragging states and beds the clearing
of rain crossing
the clearing of rain
and reiterates sleep
the absence of sleep and the absence of rain
like a book based on a cellular page
protruding or surrounding
those bodies coupled
with heather even at rest

eye

prelude

denying love's consumption, come to the gate that feeds him
the watery touch . it is not echoes shadow or the ending of
beautiful words at one with the beautiful picture, but image
denies him the ease of his mother's eyes, reflection not shadow
rejoiced in his grief knowing the other's false nature
wanted nothing but self nothing but countenance
a circle of white petals' effigy serves confusion
& mourning lacks trust . there is no modern fable
now that belief will have spirits away . the same dangers exist
as repentance is briefly a dream, likeness, merely depiction
as such is a soul who asks who is watching & written & whom
disdained in a hoped for virtue, false & true
becoming external, who are not imitation's eyes
are imitation's eyes

untitled.1

Moving these untitled permament sways
it is him not her as though meaning
were loss but pure color
you've done nothing but recover removal
past being full & recounted (like) glass
comprised of nothing Trial malignant order
Air enmeshed with movement nothing grows
in a sequence of doubt I see
the film that sees me the mark that consumes
signs like a ghost signs like a ghost
offspring shoots forth past my wanting him
Eliminate each rock that shoots forth
origin sequence outward unbound

untitled.2

Like parallel dreams the eye plunders to get up
that lasts not out of self but stays the same
same calm rigid head the shell of my sky
Sky "clot of anger" my life isn't it
a verbal ebb The last shingle
like perception's dream The divine
foreclosing sound here and there
a chair for hedonists open
Lying to what may be delivery
too soon then waking
for want of less Less time devoted
days nearer sound then saying
I'm too soon fixed as
lies lives no sooner than

untitled.3

Towards the always repeated
delicate facile origin or absolute whole
language bought in facsimile permission authority
experienced in want reproduced that
said "I'd have anything this vacant
invalid champion this waking up to morning"
As any sight or single entity entropy artifact
dim tethering can't even open the book for indecision of
images even the undemanding breech
having been left & unfrequented
need it speaks itself
My sight my mingling voice
complete

untitled.4

Anonymous impoverished under thread
as if I hadn't happened Surrender
past sleep the pale gallery
that nothing is perceived
assured the eyes the head
the mouth ears again eyes
drowning in suspension
Comes an inlet a loop as lips sealed
in pre-essence crest appears first
sub-rosa or human subordinate (to)
(a) world opens and shuts
my door adrift past
tense into the garden
to watch myself exist

untitled.5

Behold transparent house
how like a fixture unseen
for the likes of what & where
alike a greater fee for living
estranged in certain dissolute light
Entitled not to see
Withheld yet not in mimicry
that made a section of you end
Awaken all this time taken
under the opposite confused
bright transient hostage
as a hostage drips

untitled.6

Come to a grove of stems from the bottom
& go out arriving interim of break
at the crutch of day That's given work
from a table of crockery
moments of calm gravity not weight or
face that rides the byway the blossom
& crooked bloom aggrieves the wandering pass
as psalms assemble over inebriant song
Cultivate fodder farther father customs all ways
a path of stalks stuck in rain embrace solitude
not the self nor end not even age
rushing to contain these letters

untitled.7

I can't escape the mouth I'm in
Between the seer & the deep blue sea
The mirror'd road Opening
route the muted tone so clear it's
Overheard as bone white teeth
for feeling hurt enumeration
Waking from a book the book
& kin would hurt myself
"the world I'm in" holder
holder home Good thirst
or bad equilibrium
Not what breaks the
stretch of song

untitled.8

You gave a lonely song
paradox, contradiction
The border-song
octave sextet
negligible to some
beside a wall not rimmed
foreseeable future fable
a crystal replacement point by far
more temperate timed exposure
Never probed your dulled monotony
if I could walk to this door now
would open with concrete impending waste
The horn of scarcity released the wind
the wind developed brevity Oasis mocking air
primary strain set clean & dark
reducible chant that words devoted
hand fixed parts across this page

untitled.9

Who sees what wants who sees
to play to play to sleep to rhyme
Ascend the day
because a path learned
a footpath northpoint
you always point
multiple signals code
each map because
one mind presents
two and took a blade a pick
a string releasing
measure

untitled.10

To those who resemble
Can't do to whom things appear fixed
Cycle of contender doesn't kill
Don't force closed envy
By wanting to support each other
we'd throw away our other
duplicate season
Not trusting myself not to do harm to the age
No certain image is broken
Spring enfolds when winter's come
to whom things plunge
or seem as watery

untitled.11

Holding your own to delight
Love & any equal action
burst from the wreckage
Undeniably certain uneasily lost
has lost the certain always
dark green or greener self
to hand forth all sound
returning sky to touch
& touching speak
back to one's own body
Wanting nothing more unending
petal yellow white report

untitled.12

This formed evergreen
that is not evergreen
the day I spilled you
the voice often drones
a meal of first-fruits
instead of a fixture
There is no way to live without
all things arise
Arise then I tell you
the surface rings on clear
or muddy pools When these days mount
a tongue touching my other this
heard in the market
Unyielding music drones

untitled.13

Outlet in being
Curled up at call
Forestalling vote of voice
Further into non-
judgment the average quilt designed contrition
Frequent falling always truancy
into one purely lit extended shadow
pulls into secrecy
elsewhere The word source
spelling You

untitled.14

Just the image of a room
Rather than lying all together
in a concentrated animation
Or drowning to be heard
the copy of an eye
tends toward steam or vapor
The period stops enveloping
simple synaesthesia
Hyacinths begin the object maintains
last year's infrastructure
If you don't brook the difference
Like a seed

untitled.15

Minor white reflective glare
as white results with prosper
seeing doesn't exist first
measure enfold the greater loss of good
embellish what has aspects of demeanor
Base of elegy Misgiving
puncture wound worn & water
waters wanting what's
perceived is not
upon a model

untitled.16

Prompt of wanting heart's rose born earth
putting forth the object of delay
Will form this dry type of blindness
always off the table
Reading for a view to start
regarding order only who
wouldn't know their own retainer
always held a single cup
coming from that place he knows
he wants his place in

untitled.17

Clearer part of unpronounced
spread of composition Clear of
sight of things surrounding sense
as only part of disbelief
Veil & verse & misconception of
untitled body repeated motion
or fixture of a place served
already overflowed mouth that fed
pool or lily half
set sequestered

untitled.18

Who would hold me holds that device
I won't have shaken
Who says what won't be talked
is a matter of speech questioning
the central body come
to elude perdition "What I have
to deliver," the medium asked
the medium said The last rang
false true object
dangling at the bottom

untitled.19

As a vilified lake half remembering
half clock and half tower gates
if only sleeping/smoking trees
around the lake A mix of
voices sung illusion
circling leaves I'd sing
along with you

untitled.20

Hem that opaque surface
invisible on either side
Unseasoned rhetoric towards
the rise and flood
of paralyzed skin So
many sightless things
where language gets your small eye
coming as gauge
abiding your skin

untitled.21

To speak not to see to see so to listen
"Love, & be silent," sight speak self
So same as still countenance brings
Limited dumb inaudible heart
What does explain but doesn't listen
bears each thing itself
extending hand or glove the shadow
wanting waste or proof
of still white passing
more than one uncertain
fully humanized face

untitled.22

The object sees the sun
vanishing & seemingly strewn with
broken pieces held to its own
longing to address
even a hundred insistent suitors'
Missed extremities
Unconscious acquittals the present
first year opening dormant &
wanting syllables to see
a tree instead
of a leaf

untitled.23

Grass eyed ledge wandering
plunger get out of
sword to the suitor
fall in voice only
to his likeness
Not to possess whomever happened
so grieved with him
Whatever happened cast
a completing shadow in finding
he answered

untitled.24

Crossing immature tender green
emulation Because you no longer
walk a sequence wanting
the object seeking
each version pointless
white nurturing host
Progenitor's small unwavering
murmuring glass

untitled.25

Not that other body but that
fixed stupor clarity substance through
actual fields & palms & branches
of filmy odor Memory increased
or multiplied within reversed
& crossed analogy Each thing
suffers from itself where
music was infirmity alike &
falling imagery establishing
the efficiency of brief flourish

untitled.26

Bent from misgivings
points seeds or stems
Sees impediments grow
absorbing rooms or even
voices into symmetrical
waging yellow grain
Rapt antithetic answer
afflicted with human references
The occupation of a name
given for the given that
doesn't give out is wandering
rectangle the eyes
hole enliven substitute
for the rhythm of the hands
the mask enliven for the name

untitled.27

This defined obstructed ground
around the face recognized
long and rich halves deserve disorder
Scrawled insatiable outside
wanting tautology hinting
at every shade to limit
where music was like
like the configuration
of the weight of one
shadow school rocky
social breathing night
the idea of disorderly nature
The idea of consumption ending
reflection not shadow

untitled.28

A log or a rafter sprung absorption
beset or besides not sentences (or
repetition in the eyes' facsimile
the same cloth untangled
coveting as only love can
As even as day that sleeps while I sleep
moving only to build & center
motion on a spare musical
form undoing space & dissonance
which is not a small shape
held to flux between
the rib the rim precisely
that split imitation

untitled.29

Vanishes a stem to the sharpest un-
certainty a mixture of voices
reflecting surface in
the circle of leaves'
monotone to which
a hoped for external
viture and whom but confusion
serves nothing but relief
False nature but self
Nothing but countenance
A circle briefly
Depiction as such
is a who who asks who
in scattered disability

untitled.30

Insistence of dawn
to accompany or cleave
means-to-an-ends or fasten
to the goal yet not awake
not yet a secured provider
in duration "Imitation's eyes
are imitations eyes" holding
the watery front of depravation
an imperceptible touch coming
as shadow aborting shape or even room
or even fall emerging summer waging
yellow grain again

about the author

Todd Baron is the author of *Outside* (Avenue B Books), *Tell* (Texture Press), *This…Seasonal Journal* (paradigm press), *Return of the World* (O Books), *Partials* (e.g. press), *Dark as a Hat* (Abacus, Poets and Poets), and *That Looks At One and Speaks* (Factory School). In 1982 he co-founded (along with Tosh Berman) *ISSUE* magazine. In 1990 he co-founded (with Carolyn Kemp) *ReMap* Magazine. His work has appeared in various journals including *Hambone, Sulfur, Apex of the M, Temblor, Acts, New American Writing, Mandorla*, the *Washington Review, RiBot* and *The Gertrude Stein Awards for Innovative Writing* (1999). He was also one of the founding members of Littoral Books.